# Midlife

In Matthew Buckley's Smith's aptly named *Midlife*, poem after poem springs organically from exactly that — the middle of life, the middle of living, memorializing the present as they look back on childhood and forward to inevitable loss. He is the rarest of phenomenon these days, a poet who is able to use form as servant to the poem rather than its master, whose work is rich with pathos and sentiment and beauty while avoiding artificiality or cliché. These are rewarding and emotionally intelligent poems, adamantly tender and elegantly turned.

— Hailey Leithauser

"It was not beautiful," *Midlife* begins, and it is true that Matthew Buckley Smith's second collection returns again and again to failure, loss, and emptiness. Indeed, the collection thoroughly dismantles many of our dearest pieties. But what these poems desecrate, we come to realize, should never have been sacred — a comforting lie is still a lie and more dangerous for its comfort. Nor is Smith all despair or simply a misanthrope. For all their formal, rational precision, these poems care most about human beings, and their concern honors our hardships. As Smith attends to our personal and collective disappointments, he does so with such extraordinary eloquence, such nimble rhythm and rhyme, such marvelously incisive details, that we find ourselves smiling even as we are taken apart. This book is hard and generous and very beautiful.

— George David Clark

. . . virtuosic formal facility, as well as the nimble elegance of his classically plain style . . . .

— Brian Brodeur, *Spoon River Poetry Review*

# MIDLIFE

by

Matthew Buckley Smith

Measure Press
Savannah, Georgia

The text of this book is composed in OFL Sorts Mill Goudy.
Composition by R.G.
Jacket Design by Daniel Alexander Smith

Buckley Smith, Matthew
 Midlife / by Matthew Buckley Smith — 1st ed.

ISBN-13: 978-1-939574-38-1
ISBN-10: 1-939574-38-2
Library of Congress Control Number: 2023945619


Cover Art by Daniel Alexander Smith

Measure Press
2 Longberry Lane
Savannah, GA 31419
http://www.measurepress.com/measure/

## Acknowledgements

Thanks are due to the editors of the following journals where these poems first appeared, sometimes in earlier versions:

| | |
|---|---|
| *32 Poems* | *Literary Matters* |
| *Able Muse Review* | *New Ohio Review* |
| *AGNI* | *Poetry Northwest* |
| *American Arts Quarterly* | *Raintown Review* |
| *Angle* | *Rattle* |
| *At Length* | *Smartish Pace* |
| *Beloit Poetry Journal* | *Southern Poetry Review* |
| *Birmingham Poetry Review* | *Spillway* |
| *Classical Outlook* | *Subtropics* |
| *Commonweal* | *Threepenny Review* |
| *Ecotone* | *You Are the River: Literature Inspired by* |
| *Harvard Review* | *the North Carolina Museum of Art* |
| *Linebreak* | |

Thanks also to the following poets, whose poems I imitated in my own: Catullus (and Paul McCartney) in "Hail and Farewell"; Horace in "Drinking Ode" and "Political Ode"; Ashley Anna McHugh in "Sleeping Dogs"; Rilke in "Archaic Torso of Aphrodite"; Sappho (and Catullus) in "Doubt"; and A.E. Stallings in "Odysseus' Mother Greets Her Son in Hell."

This book had a long road to publication, and I owe a debt to the many people who helped it along the way: to David Yezzi for picking the manuscript for the Richard Wilbur Award; to Paul Bone and Rob Griffith for rescuing it from publishing oblivion after the first publisher collapsed; to everyone who provided help and encouragement throughout its composition, including Dan Brown, Chris Childers, Clark Cloyd, Maryann Corbett, Joseph Cullen, Nick Friedman, J.P. Gritton, Mark Mansfield, Michael McFee, Josh Mehigan, the Meringoff family, Burt Myers, Alex Pepple, Zara Raab, Mary Jo Salter, Eric Smith, Alicia Stallings, Ernie Suarez, Mark Strand, Daniel Wallace, Able Muse Review & Press, The Association of Literary Scholars, Critics, and

Writers, The Paideia School, The Sewanee Writers' Conference, and The West Chester Poetry Conference; to Brian Brodeur for reviewing a book that did not yet exist and to David Clark, Hailey Leithauser, Shane McCrae, Mary Jo Salter, Alan Shapiro, and David Yezzi for blurbing it; to Ernie Hilbert for offering practical advice on its design and to Daniel Smith for designing it; to all the lovely, generous, sometimes maddening people I've come to know — or know better — through *SLEERICKETS*, especially Alice, Brian, and Cameron, for the kindness they showed me when this book looked like a goner (NB: I promise there are no prose poems in this book and only one sestina, which you have my permission to skip); to Jonathan Farmer and Alan Shapiro for their constant moral and editorial support, particularly during the last year of writing; to my vast and patient family for continuing to put up with me; to Ryan Wilson — teacher, reader, brother, friend — for more good turns than would be prudent to mention; and most of all to my three best girls — Josie, Ellie, and Joanna.

for Joanna
*sine qua non*

# CONTENTS

She wanted to die, and also to live in Paris.
— *Madame Bovary*

# The Year of

It was not beautiful.
It did not rhyme.
A brick came loose.
A text message came late.
We lacked the understanding
then the time
to put things straight.
Results were lost.
Releases went unsigned.
Defective units
had already sold.
The smaller demographics fell behind.
The trail went cold.
A judge enforced
the nondisclosure form.
The damage wasn't
covered by the plan.
The girl got
transferred to a different dorm.
The threats began.
Some children
were too young to understand.
A biopsy was needed
to confirm.
The prototype regrettably
was manned.
Budgets were short-term.
Though we were brave,

though we were dutiful,
not all of us were
fitted for the climb.
It was not fair.
It was not beautiful.
It did not rhyme.

I.

# Object Permanence

Because you haven't yet developed faith
That what you see at nightfall will return
At dawn, when time begins again, it's death
    You nightly learn

To dread, like the recurrence of a dream
In which your father or your mother stands
And takes you (singing every time the same
    Unmeaning sounds)

Upstairs into the reeling hall that slides
With horrifying slowness toward that room
Peopled with deaf-mute mammals on all sides,
    Dim as the womb,

Where you are left to beg and, helpless, watch
As warmth and human touch and hope retreat
Into the dark, which, closing with a latch,
    Becomes complete.

No one can hear, but you cry anyway
For more time in the world you hardly knew,
Here in the body one momentous day
    We loved as you.

# Sleeping Dogs

When we hear the news your neighbor shot herself,
I'm slow to link her name to the smiling face
We see every Christmas at your parents' place
And each morning on our fridge, dressed as an elf.

Strange that two girls who grew up a block apart
Share little but a birthplace anymore —
Just a spare key that you kept to her front door
And an old phone number you still know by heart.

These days you've got me: to love you, not to die,
To try to keep in warm, vague, tender doubt
Some certainties that we don't talk about,
To wash the plates and stow them when they're dry,

Or just to shake the water from a knife
And take you in my dripping arms for now,
Shushing the questions gathered at your brow
About the kind of person who ends her life.

For you I keep that silence. For your friend
I offer to the silence where she went
The hope that what she did is what she meant
And what she knew of pain is at an end.

# Requited Love

Here is the way they rose and bathed and fed
In silence, and in silence got undressed,
And microwaved the supper each thought best,
And meant the words the TV actors said.
Here is her naked hand outstretched in bed
To soothe some restless memory's knocking chest,
And here her present body, seldom pressed
Awake to his, and here his snoring head.
Here are the things they thought they had to fear —
The figure at the far end of a glance,
Neglected taxes, mice, the common cold,
The lovely hair's retreat, the veins' advance,
The skulls a little clearer every year,
Shares held too long, the child they'd never hold.

# Hail and Farewell

Of course you'd pick a place where they don't serve beer.
One flight, two shitty boat rides, three month's pay
Palmed out in petty bribes to get me here,
And I can't afford to stay more than a day.
Remember that song Dad liked — *You say goodbye,*
*I say hello* — how he'd draw out every word
When he sang it in the car? *Hello, hello!*
I've had it in my head ever since I heard.
*Goodbye, I don't know why . . .*

                          Well, I have to go.
If Dad were here, he'd know just what to say,
Something to do with the dust and wind and sun,
Something that's not a lie or a cliché,
But I'm not Dad, and you're not anyone.
You can't hear a word I say. I don't know why.

# Regret

The things we thought best
Left undone
I haven't confessed
To anyone,

And all we kept
Ourselves from when
We turned and slept
Apart has been

Hushed with the phrase
We never said
And all the ways
We spoke instead

And just how well
We knew, and why,
The truths we would tell,
The untold lie.

# Briar and Rose

The little, the less, the nothing we could do
For the princess asleep between the sleeping walls,
And whether it mattered, and whether our hearts were true,
　　No one recalls.

Between the sleeping walls, the kitchen sleeps,
The throne room, and the staircase by the door,
All night the sleeping candles cast their shapes
　　On the sleeping floor.

The aged king sleeps on treaties at his desk,
In her bath the queen sleeps canopied in steam,
The princess sleeps without her sleeping mask
　　And does not dream.

She does not dream of us asleep outside,
Where we hang, pinioned by the poison briar,
Dangling in the same chain mail in which we died
　　Full of desire,

Where we'll hang until the sleepers part their eyes,
When a young man just like us but more in luck
Arrives, and everything we could not seize
　　He'll timely pluck.

# Voyeurs

We envied first the eyes he'd make
At her whenever she would break

Some troubled silence with a squeal
That proved our lapsing patter fake.

The way he'd rise to fill her wine,
You claimed, and then again recline

Against her breast, began to take
The fun out of refreshing mine.

For weeks I wished to sleep beside
Her figure, frank and tipsy-eyed.

For him your sigh became a sign
To translate, had he ever tried.

Just once, after some half-drunk meal,
We let the jokes and cake congeal

And, hushed for seconds, ceased to hide
The longing we no longer feel.

# The Best

You're wrong, she said,
if you think I don't recall
the drive we made at the end,
from Hartwell to Jasper,
across that summer's last
long weekend, fall
a sobering whisper.
When did we start
to fool ourselves out loud?
You went first, but I
don't hold it against you.
You were so handsome
then, and I was so proud,
though I never convinced you.
A little farther on
was all I wanted,
in the white compact,
humming some aimless song.
I sold it last year. My fiancé
said it was haunted,
and he wasn't wrong.
He's shorter than you, and better
with his hands, and better.
You wouldn't like him,
but he might still like you.
His ex was a beauty, I hear,
though I never met her,
or wanted to.

I'm almost glad
things went the way they did —
the last drive west,
the last fuck by the water,
the last big lie, the best.
Now I hear you have a kid,
a beauty, a daughter.

# The Light of the Body

You're here. I knew you'd make it. Come on in.
Coffee? Iced tea? No trouble either way.
You know the other afternoon at Tanger
When — just like that — you walked up and said hi?
That meant the world to me, it truly did.
You wouldn't believe the way some people act.
The credit analysts, the other tellers —
You'd think they never met me in their life.
You're the exception. You're exceptional.
The way you smiled, like not a thing had changed,
It made me wish I'd done more at the time
To get to know you. I regret so much,
More what I didn't do than what I did.
But now you're here, now we've got all this time.

Well, why don't I just come right out and say it?
You must have seen the pictures. I don't mind.
I mean, I did back then. I couldn't bear
The thought that everyone at work had seen.
Those things we did were never my idea.
I thought I loved him. I thought he loved me.
I thought he'd be the one to give me babies.
Still, don't fret. Anybody would have looked.
When we broke up, he sent those pictures out
Not just to everybody at the bank,
But Mom and Dad and all my girlfriends too,
My neighbors, my old classmates, anyone
Whose name was in my laptop or my phone.

The day it all came out, I called in sick,
Turned off my phone, and drove out of the city.

Back in high school I used to know a girl
Who lived up here. Sometimes I'd stay the night
And Sunday come along with her to church.
For them, church was a castle made of glass,
Announced by this big blinking golden sign,
Lit up each week with some new verse from scripture:
To you these things were shown that you might know!
When the eye is clear the body fills with light!
For now we look into a darkened mirror
But soon shall see each other face to face!
That awful day I drove around for hours
Praying for some suggestion of His plan,
Some clue that I was more than how I looked
In all those pictures everybody saw,
A hint that what they'd seen — my body, made
Public in every wrinkle, mole, and hair —
That it might still be worth something to someone.
The sun was fading when I saw the sign,
Its golden light still blinking by the church:
God saw what he had made and it was good.
That afternoon, I put in my two weeks.
I broke my lease in town and got this place,
A fifteen-minute walk down to the church
Where I became Director of Youth Worship.

The kids are great, fourteen to eighteen, mostly,
So fragile at that stage, in flux, in pain,
All hung up between longing and disgust,
Careless with one another and themselves,

More beautiful than they will ever know.
I love them. And I love them all the more
Now that I've stopped pursuing my desires
And started letting God decide my path.
I once believed that I was meant to be
A wife, a mother, someone with a family,
And in a funny way I wasn't wrong.
It's not the path I would have picked myself,
But you and I both saw where that path ends.

Speaking of which, last week, before you saw me —
Just a few minutes earlier — I saw you.
I'd stepped into the hallway just outside
That little curtained row of fitting rooms,
And as I passed, the air swept back a curtain,
Baring a strip of mirror for an instant
And with it your small body in the light,
Half-bending to pick up a bathing suit
Puddled there on the little pleather bench.
I saw then what He wanted me to see:
That He had made you lovely to behold,
That you and I are sisters, that you're loved,
That something made as lovingly as you
Was not meant for destruction after death.
He sees us all, He numbers every hair,
He marks the fall of every little bird —

Please don't get up. I didn't mean to scare you.
You're free to go. I never lock my door.
But please, first, take a moment, take a breath,
And ask yourself: Why did you make this drive —
Out of the city, past the outlet malls,

The airport, all those miles of dying farms?
Why did you come here to this rust-stained knot
Of ugly brick apartments, to this room,
To check in on some former coworker,
A girl whose name you only half-remembered?
Ask yourself: Who was leading you to me?
You see the truth, inside you've always seen.
Now close your eyes. He's with us. Let us pray.

# Chez Bovary

I should not say this here
And wouldn't if I thought you'd listen somewhere else,
            Behind the bedroom's blank,
Shut blinds, perhaps, or in the kitchen over a glass
            Of something cool and clear,
Or outside, walking underneath the poplars, damp leaves
            Bruised and bandage-lank,
Or wherever one is meant to say what one believes:

            The life you long for isn't
The wrong life, necessarily, for you to long for,
            But it's not the one we've made
Here, where we've stopped, with no one else to stop
        being young for,
            In this dim burg, imprisoned,
As you seem, every night when I get home, to be,
            Taking again to bed
For weeks, for months, for all the long hours casually

            Agreed to some time back,
When you were not, or still thought you were not, yet past
            All of the magic youth
Persuades us to accept as real, as real at least
            As the terrifying lack
Of magic middle age reveals. My love, my small,
            Smart, nervous girl, the truth
You would not hear is this: We're dying.
                            That is all.

# Elizabethan

*for E.*

This winter, your first and only without English,
Without memories or means yet to remember,
The world looks small which you'll discover endless
Between tonight and this time next December,

As every intervening day convinces
Your tongue to love this language of the dead,
Impressive terms pronounced by Norman princes,
Along with stuff the Saxon forebears said,

And all the grounds and evergreens without
The mortgaged walls I sing to you within
Take on a breadth they lacked the day we bought
The plot with which your story would begin,

Likewise, these lines I've taken pains to measure,
Should they live long enough to bring you pleasure.

2.

# Undergrads

The place we lived was only an idea,
Nothing to do with the failed cotton mill town
Where a record shop, some bars, and a pizzeria
Were all we ever cared to call our own.
From nightmares of a happy life with kids
We'd wake in boozy sweat to find the floor
Still cobbled with bottle caps and take-out lids,
Our twenties crumpled safely in a drawer,
Unspent like all the hours ahead that night
We found each other in the common room
And made somehow without the help of light
Our way across the river by the time
Dawn spilled down from the campus to the banks
We came to, single, sobered-up again,
To see the morning glories give their thanks
For things we had, and hardly noticed, then.

# Ars Poetica

We watched the plant somebody left with us
Elbow its pair of buds into the room
For days, in pursed, white-throated, partial bloom,
Until the small one, mocking Icarus,
Spread its sun-plaited blessings for an hour
And dropped, burnt-feathered, lusterless, agape,
Down to the floor we never swept, its shape
Let tumble like a body from a tower.
The larger bud, more patient, peers down still,
Untrimmed by sun or shears or busy time,
Keeping a height no second chance will climb,
A promise only bided time can kill.

# Lenox Square

*for B.*

How is it for them now, the ones who stayed
Behind us in that place we used to work?
Still name-tagged, still clocked-in-and-out, still paid
   By the same jerk,

The way we were back then, the year we took
The same job at the same store for a lark.
How many times did we sell the same joke,
   Curse the same dark?

I learned to fold a dress shirt and to dress
Like you, expensively, slightly askew.
We spent more than we meant and took home less.
   Girls took home you.

The last time we ditched early for a slice
At the mid-town patio with dollar pours,
We must have killed a pack or more apiece,
   A dozen Coors.

That was eight years ago and feels like eight.
We both have better jobs now, and worse clothes,
And others to ask for love. Ask yours. It's late,
   And time to close.

# Doo-Wop

This is the sound
The drunk heart makes
After it's drowned
A life's mistakes,

The tonic chord
Of a dead quartet
That love ignored
But can't forget,

Who keen and hum
And call not sense
But feeling from
Indifference,

And something true
From the empty air,
And thoughts of you
From anywhere.

# Egg and Dart

*for R.*

Here in the studio, everything has its place
And every man his tools and given task.
I am the one that makes the egg-and-dart.
Outsiders seldom recognize the term:
It names the trim on certain walls and columns,
Sometimes around the edge of a relief,
That alternates an oval with a bar
Forever in a perfect marble band
The excellence of which is not being seen.
You have not seen it many times before.
Next time, perhaps, you will not think of me,
The nobody who gives this nothing shape,
The oldest in our studio by far,
Apart from the old master — just my senior,
As in the first days, by a few short years,
The length of an apprenticeship for most.

The master's own apprenticeship concluded,
Perhaps too early, with a masterpiece:
A seraph in a doorway gazing on
A child Madonna shrouded like a crone,
Her misery suspended by the word
The angel brings of joy soon to be born,
And soon thereafter fixed upon a cross.
The scene was carved from one pink marble slab,
The maker hardly older than the maid.
It is a wonder. Go sometime and see.

Four decades since have not produced the like.
Such is my master's failure, justly grand,
As mine is justly slight enough to keep
Within the margins where I've made a life
Of egg-and-dart-and-egg-and-dart-and-egg.
Sometimes a serif or a curlicue
Alters the line, a blossom now and then,
Brief variations on a constant theme.
I make the new boys practice till they weep.
For them I'm yet no different than the master,
Another beard, another marble hand.
The older ones know better. Egg-and-dart
They loathe, and gladly shirk, and cannot think
Of anything but being soon beyond it.
They make good sport of me: The Knave of Darts,
Methuselah, the Master's Wife, his Mother.
Each cohort think their cleverness the first.

Some have, it's true, known something of success.
A few have set up workshops of their own,
Contending for commissions now with us —
Dull, churchy tableaux mostly, gaudy stuff
Fit only for the pious and the rich.
Not one of them has yet achieved a piece
Like that with which our master made his name,
And none could ever chisel egg-and-dart
More than a pace or two, and those two false,
The darts strung loose, no pair of eggs the same.
Though some lacked cunning, most lacked only care,
And even when I made them watch my hands
Shaping a path across the element,
None of them saw the Knave of Darts himself.

If any had, he might have seen a man
At home within the shadow of a man,
Content to turn out faultlessly his craft
For children's pay and incidental thanks.
No wonder they look elsewhere for their dreams.

My own, of late, touch on the blessed Virgin,
Mantled in pink, just as our master made her
The day he drew the rubble from her face
And found her flushed with motherly despair,
Compelled to carry what she might not keep.
I pray that she will guide the master's hand
One final time, for one last worthy form,
A miracle to warm his dying fame,
A garment of which I might take the hem.

This morning, though, no mysteries are revealed.
Fleeing an endless breakfast with the count
To play a prince among apprentices,
Our master has declared, perhaps in jest,
That Egg and Dart are meant to signify
The figures of a Woman and a Man,
Begetting undistinguished generations
One undistinguished coupling at a time.
An older boy, restless to show his wit,
Suggests that Egg and Dart are Eye and Tongue,
Perceptive and appetitive in turn,
Enshackled by a mutual disdain.
The quips and quibbles patter on and on,
And not a word I haven't heard before.

Now we will lose the working day to talk

Of women's tongues and men's relentless eyes.
Wine will be brought, a boy will play guitar.
No one will think to ask me what I think.
For forty years I've cut the egg, the dart.
I've never known a woman or a man
As I have them, not my own eyes and tongue.
I know what they are. I know what they're not.
If asked I'd say they are nothing less than stone.

# Archaic Torso of Aphrodite

Rilke looked at a torso of Apollo
And heard the sentence *You must change your life.*

Profound advice, if difficult to follow:
Life has a way of reasserting life,

And if a broken god can still retain
His godlike powers and his godlike plans,

A man's life, no less fragile, no less vain,
Though changed for good will always be a man's.

Consider, then, this marble Aphrodite,
Still beautiful despite her missing parts,

Still recognizable as Aphrodite,
Still, even broken, fit for breaking hearts,

As if unchanged.
               And yet, she seems to say
To you, who look too long, *Friend, look away.*

# Nostalgia

The streetlamp paints the leaves
Beyond the parking lot with gold, familiar light —
Dull, homely, local vines,
But from the sidewalk, through the settling darkness, sight,
Like memory, misbehaves,
And their strands almost compose the shuddering ivy wall
That hid all posted signs
And warnings on the street you lived on that last fall.
I know already why,
Odd hours, odd places, even now the years give way
And open on that scene:
Clay-rusted asphalt, moss yard, wooden house, each day
A green, perpetually
Hungover proxy for intoxicated night.
The things that might have been
Invariably matter more the less they might,
Which now is not at all,
As you must know and I continually forget
And others now the age
(Sweet, stumbling, shy) we were back then have not learned ye
Who'd envy them their fall?
Or the man who isn't me the nights he shares
Somewhere with you? Or grudge
These leaves the dateless light they're burning in like years?

# Political Ode

Let Varius be the one who writes the song,
    Agrippa, of your latest victory.
He's as brave in verse as you are in a throng
    Of foreign men-at-arms or cavalry.

Just ask Maecenas: I'm not one to sing
    Of such grave matters as Achilles' wrath
Or poor Ulysses' crooked piloting
    Or Agamemnon's hot homecoming bath.

A poet of my humble luck, beholden
    To friends and patrons for his cup and plate,
Is not the sort the Muses dare embolden
    To outline any politician's fate.

Let others paint the leaders of our time,
    Dressed out like Mars in adamantine arms
Or like Meriones in Trojan grime
    Or Diomedes in Minerva's charms.

My war songs are the anthems of the bored,
    The heroes of my less-than-epic tales
Old fools like me, who've scarcely held a sword,
    Whose scars are all from happy housewives' nails.

# Drinking Ode

*for R.*

Drink with me, old man — there's no time
And no use trying to be good.
Our flesh was supple, our thoughts sublime,
And now death eats us alive, and should.
The gods aren't missing any sleep
Over the altar lights we burn
To honor afterlives we keep
Pretending we might someday earn.
The king, the peasant farmer, even
You and I and everyone,
Can pick the suit we'd like to leave in
But not the day the tailor's done.
So cowards survive the battlefield
And bullies fill the lifeboats first
And rich kids get their records sealed,
But some verdicts can't be reversed.
Men say a river worms around
The grove where dead souls speak again,
But that black swamp has long since drowned
Both ferryboat and ferryman.
Your land, your house, your tender wife,
The plum trees planted by your hand —
You'll leave them when you leave this life
For a ditch beneath a cypress stand,
And the man who takes your place will spill
Your choicest vintage wine onto
The white jacquard chaise longue you still
Believe somehow belongs to you.

# Another Achilles

Better, my mother always said, to be
The servant of a servant here on earth
Than king among the dead. Wise words, perhaps,
From one who never had to rule, or serve.
Myself, I had the fortune to be born
A king, or king-to-be, among the living.
Today, my father long deceased, I sit
Here on his throne, in Phthia, growing plump
With sunny trade and endless golden weather,
Leading with soft, pale, patient hands a tribe
Of shepherds, farmers, vintners, and the like.
Our milkmaids are the pride of Thessaly,
Our walnut baklava the stuff of dreams.
It is a good life. I am a good king.

My wife, a gentle stout Euboean girl
Whose dowry brought a hundred head of kine
Looks after me as sweetly as a mother
And mothers like a wife our dozen boys.
They're grown and bearded all, but still at home,
Unmarried and without a taste for war.
I love them, lazy creatures that they are,
Although I've ruined them. By now it's plain
No king of any honorable city
Would ever leave a daughter in their hands.
When I am dead, they'll break the kingdom up
Till everything my father proudly built
Is counted, joist by nail, and sold for parts.

All things, he used to say, must have an end.
My own, like me, will be forgettable.
There will come other kingdoms, other kings.
I cannot claim the gods have given me
A single drachma less than my desert.

Yet sometimes, for all that, I rise at night,
Disoriented in the darkened room,
Thinking that I've awakened somewhere else,
My red silk sheets a simple woolen sack,
The bedroom walls a battered canvas tent,
My wife's bronze looking glass a glinting shield,
And outside not a whispering Phthian breeze
But the Aegean's unrelenting tide.
I lie in shadow, trying to recall
The place I'm in and in it my own place,
Until a kindly wind unclouds the moon,
Restoring bed and vanity and wife,
And once again I'm nothing but myself,
Achilles, ruler of the Myrmidons,
Another of his generation's sons
Born to a father greater than himself,
Though one of just a few who in his youth
Showed prudence and refused to sail to Troy,
Where every last Achaean ship was torched
And every man, horse, slave, and concubine
Cut down and buried in the muddy surf
Under the gleaming chariots of Priam.
It didn't feel like prudence at the time.

I'd heard the rumors that the Argive king
Was gathering a force of demigods

To sack the richest city in the world.
My father and my mother heard them, too.
The old man would have sailed once more for glory,
Had all his oft-recounted feats of arms
Not ground away his pith and left him lame,
But in his place he charged me to set sail,
Taking his horses and his ashen spear
Along with every man of fighting age
To haul back ships half-sunk with Trojan loot.
Proud Peleus. He was too old to hear
Whatever words I might have wished to say,
So I said none, but kissed his hand and left.
That night my mother smuggled me to Skyros.

There on the island, I was draped in silk
And hidden with the daughters of the king.
My mother was a superstitious soul,
And one night on the island she confessed
The gods had granted me a double fate,
That, should I choose to take the favored path,
My name would live three thousand years and more
Though for my body less than ten remained,
And so another path was offered me,
Less honorable, less painful, more obscure,
Down which I'd know prosperity and pleasure,
A wife, a grassy countryside, a throne,
And when the great god Hermes came at last
To lead me to the darkness, my reward
Would be an absolute oblivion
On earth as in the kingdom of the dead.
For her there was no question of a choice.
She wanted only for her son to live.

And so I lived on Skyros as a girl
Where every market stall and kitchen thrummed
With whispers of young men who'd sailed to Aulis,
Intent on battle, plunder, and revenge
Against the preening horsemen of the east.
The legends flowed, and then began to ebb.
The girls and eunuchs gossiped less and less,
And I believed the time to choose had passed.

One afternoon a little boat appeared,
Oared by an ancient hunchback, heaped with trunks
Of pottery and clothing and perfume.
The other girls, bored, curious, went to see.
Most of the stock was cheap or chipped or frayed,
But as the others started to disperse,
I noticed, propped beside a spool of yarn,
A shield of wood and leather, bossed in bronze,
And, lying just beside it in the sand,
A polished spear, tipped with a leaf-shaped blade.
I took one step, unthinking, hand outstretched,
And just below the peddler's cloak I saw
The taut calf of an athlete in his prime
Contracting slowly, like a bow drawn back,
And from the shadows of the old man's cowl
There gleamed a grinning row of straight white teeth.
I turned my scented back and walked away,
Hurrying up the strand to find my place
Among the patient flock of palace girls,
Ready to give myself to the diversions
The eunuchs had devised for us that day —
Perhaps a footrace or a game of darts.
I've always shown a talent for such things.
When I looked back, Odysseus was gone.

3.

# Odysseus' Mother Greets Her Son in Hell

I thought I'd meet you here, though not like this:
Some dead boy-soldier's favorite sword in hand.
I thought you'd be dead too, yet here you stand,
Face weary with the world I thought you'd miss.
When is it mothers lose their sons to men,
To filthy jokes and theories of attack?
Even in death, we never get you back.
A killer can't become a child again.
Please, stop your shouting. I still know my name,
And I can almost call yours from the dark,
A pretty one, the girls used to remark.
Down here all words begin to sound the same.
It pains me that I can't remember, though,
The lullaby you always wanted sung
When you were small and scared, and I was young.
Whatever was it called? How did it go?

# Lullaby Before Birth

For now you can be happy,
Whatever you are called,
A thing no hands have held,
In darkness, where you wait
And nothing soon will stop you
Unfastening the gate.

Come through and you will find us
And cry until you can't,
And every day you count
A gift will be a loan,
And all the dark beyond us
Someday will be your own.

So stay a little longer
Where morning isn't yet
And nothing is too late,
And all the rest will keep.
We grow, but never younger,
And have no time to sleep.

# Posterity

The great remembered man whose name is stone
Over the double doors where students pass
Today is remembered for his name alone,
   On the way to class,

By those whose names, being something less than great,
Someday will be remembered even less,
By others, also young and running late,
   In different dress,

And then, as now, sunlight will mark the lawn
And August will sigh the syllable of fall,
Considering the generations gone
   Scarcely at all,

As scarcely as we consider those to come,
Among our busy thoughts of work and rest,
As scarcely as the seedling in the womb
   Considers the breast,

Which you, no longer shy, bare to the day,
Here on this quiet campus garden bench,
For our girl, who soon enough will thirst in a way
   We cannot quench.

# The End

You want your bedtime story
told, not read,
meaning you want it made up
on the spot,
so, sitting at the corner
of your bed, I tug my beard,
and stall, and like as not
begin the tale with
"Once upon a time . . ."
and introduce a girl
about your age,
locked in a tower far
too tall to climb
or in a golden-
barred, unbending cage,
from which she must
in order to escape
employ both wit
and heart, making
new friends and losing
old ones as the end
takes shape, wherein
a message, or a marriage, tends
to leave the kingdom's
fictive doors ajar,
as if awaiting someone.
As they are.

# The Octonauts

*Perhaps. We'll see. Be patient. I don't know.*
By now you're old enough
to understand
each is a different way
of saying no
to your most recent
teary-eyed demand,
be it for one
more hour of TV,
a new house and a husband
of your own, or wings
that let you flutter like a bee.
*Not yet. Maybe someday.*
*Wait till you're grown.*
So when you calmly asked
the other day
*Will we still be a family*
*when we're dead?*
I kissed you, swept
a loose eyelash away,
and in my softest grownup
whisper said,
while turning on your favorite
TV show,
*Perhaps. We'll see. Be patient. I don't know.*

# Anniversaries

The day now seems a happy accident,
To which the two survivors lift a drink,
And share, since greasy takeout's too much money,
Sex and old cake. She tears up, still a girl
With months of glowering interest on her hand,
Who finally has her cake. Who's not alone.

Too often they wake, dress, and eat alone.
When both are home it's a kind of accident.
In bed she yelps, once, at his sleepy hand,
Thinking it a mouse. He likes to drink,
But waits till she's asleep. There's no other girl.
They both work hard, and one of them makes money.

The part they talk about the least is money.
Neither one grew up hungry, and each alone
Would hardly starve, but when the waiter's a girl
He always grabs the check. By accident,
One night, or since she's had a second drink,
She slaps it out of his school-teaching hand.

In their worst fight he's never raised a hand,
Though he has wanted to. It's not the money,
It's that ever since he learned which wine to drink,
He can't remember, tipsy and alone,
How he lived once — rent a monthly accident,
Each night the same bar and a different girl.

It's longer, so he tells the checkout girl,
The list of what she cannot eat or drink,
Than the list of what she can. He shops alone.
As she pretends to nap, remote in hand,
He takes the keys and sunglasses and money
And daydreams of a one-car accident.

One night a year they drink with a free hand
While a girl watches the kids for pizza money.
Alone, some years, they seem no accident.

# Elegy Without Consolation

When you are very old and I am dead
And silence fills the pages of our bed

And strangers wear the things I used to fold
And neither sons nor sleep can blunt the cold,

When every hour a different faucet leaks
And somebody keeps moving the antiques

And days collect on windowsills, and years,
And what is yours of beauty disappears,

When you extend your hand to find at dawn
The names for watch and keys and wallet gone

And all the letters littering this page
Are hieroglyphics from another age,

Take time to linger on the white below
These words of comfort others seem to know.

# The Quick

Today you amount to little
more than names,
Lois and Bertha Clark,
here in the world
you waited for,
on which you hardly
left a mark,
just two plots settled
in the shade of a cypress,
where you still await
parents who twice
in one year paid
for a slab
with a single name
and date.

# Natural Prosody

*for* C.C.

The late September afternoons decline,
The same, almost, as twenty years ago.
A younger man might take it as a sign,
The way I took the clean iambic line
My ninth-grade English teacher stood below,
"The láte Septémber áfternóons declíne."
Mr. C., favorite of many and of mine,
Loved poems more than a poet, so much so
A younger man might take it as a sign.
Most lights are meant to wink, and not to shine,
He told us, laughing as he let us know
*The late September afternoons decline*
Was his own work, a single verse, and fine,
His one example, one *ex animo* —
A younger man might take it as a sign.
Some disappointments happen by design,
Things grow a while, and then they cease to grow.
The late September afternoons decline.
A younger man might take it as a sign.

# Survey of Love

The Greeks believe that Love was born the day
Time sickled off the testicles of Heaven

And flung them out into the ocean's spray,
Which gives back altered everything it's given.

The Norse say Love is feathered like a hawk,
That when she weeps her tears are purest gold,

That she may meet her death at Ragnarok,
Though never can she marry or grow old.

The Christians teach that love is giving up
Yourself for others, this world for the next —

A stiff drink from a dead carpenter's cup,
A tax collector's duty to the taxed.

But you, you say love's no more than a word
Less often heard than hoped for, meant than heard.

# The Fell Swoop

I guess you've probably googled me by now.
You should. These days a girl can't be too careful.
Tonight, though, you're in luck. I'm very nice.
That's what the neighbors say, or most of them,
In certain articles you would have seen:
*A shock ... A tragedy ... The nicest man ...*
Now, to be fair, a handful disagreed,
Including some that I'd considered friends.
They snatched the chance to speculate in public,
"Translating" body language, trading memes,
And peddling their unlikely explanations
Of what I did, of what they think I am.
But let me ask you what I've asked myself:
How many of those amateur detectives
Can say they ever truly loved their families
The way I loved my own?

                       I wish you'd caught
The TV interview I gave last spring
When I addressed the kidnapper directly:
*You cannot grasp the nature of my love.*
The footage is on YouTube, so I'm told.
The other week it topped a million views.
Still, in the end, it hardly made a difference.
No phone call came. No ransom note arrived.
No jogger happened on a heap of corpses.
And even that night, early in the search,
As I stood fast and faced the rolling cameras

To read the written statement of my love,
I sensed it — that my wife and our fine boys
Were all already gone, and that no words
Would ever call them home to me again.

Are you all right? You've hardly touched your food.
Please, eat. I'll order us another bottle.
Now, what were we discussing? Yes, the past.
Someone as young as you can't understand,
Not really, what it means to have regrets,
But by the time you're my age you'll have learned
That certain choices can't be taken back,
And that eventually we all endure
Two lives: the life we greet each day on waking,
And then the life we wake to in our dreams.
I used to dream that, had I been on time
For that last round of callbacks in '03,
Had I turned down the steady retail job
And said yes to the unpaid internship
In that experimental midtown playhouse
And left the following fall for New York City
And not for Maryland's third-best school of law,
Or had I simply married someone else,
Or nobody at all, and had no kids —
And, yes, if mostly I had had no kids —
I might have made a life upon the stage,
Playing the roles that every actor longs for:
Brick and Orestes, Oedipus and Hickey,
Hamlet, Iago, Brutus, Lear, MacDuff.
That kind of life, a dream-life free of dreams,
It seems beyond the limits of the body,
A feat you couldn't possibly achieve . . .

Until the day you open up the *Times*
And, just like that, atop the Culture section
Some kid grins at you, double-fisting Tonys,
Who used to snap the ball to you in school.

I'm sorry. I've been rambling. You're too young —
Happily *much* too young — to understand
The pain of watching other people live
A life that by all rights should be your own.
But standing in the studio that night,
Speaking the speech about my poor dead family
Whose deaths had not — still haven't — been confirmed,
I caught my own reflection in the lens,
A handsome man, a man not yet too old
To sell his house and rent a small apartment,
Take acting lessons, build a résumé,
Lose weight, buy Rogaine, sleep with twenty-somethings,
And be the man he always meant to be.
I saw this new life taking shape before me
As I appealed for mercy to the man
Whom I had so consistently described
To county, state, and federal detectives . . .
A man who, surely, has his own regrets.
Now *there's* a thought to put an end to sleep.

Well, I'll be damned! We've made it to dessert.
This place — trust me — you really can't go wrong.
I've tried it all, and nothing disappoints:
The frosted figs, the caramel meringue,
The rhubarb tart, the salted creme brulée!
If anything, you'll want to try it all.
So take a breath, look over every choice,

And if, somehow, you don't like what you get,
Remember that it's not too late to change.
You know the secret to a happy life?
It's not too late. It never is too late.

# Philomela

It ended sooner than a song,
The thing he did without a word.
They hadn't known each other long.
It ended sooner than a song,
And no one seemed to think it wrong:
She was not changed into a bird.
It ended sooner than a song,
The thing he did without a word.

4.

# Carmen Barbarorum

Our fathers sacked this city
That someday all their children might be princes of it:
The gates of broken marble,
The long, wracked columns, the senate floor, bare sky above it,
The rich, obscene graffiti,
Mute gods and mottos to which daily we grow deafer,
The lintels cut with horrible,
Heroic names even our shamans can't decipher.
Best not to understand
These relics of a decadent taskmaster race,
Those who so long enthralled
Our kind with fiscal sleight of hand and martial grace,
Their spiky ramparts manned,
Summer, fall, winter, spring, by ironclad legionnaires,
Watched in turn by the fat, bald,
Perfume-beribboned sons of bald, fat emperors.
Less noble, we are better,
A simple truth we teach our children to repeat:
Our sins briefer and slighter,
Our public things more free, our public more complete,
No child born to a fetter,
No man run through for spectators, no hearth gone cold
And no hearth burning brighter,
No god but good, no worldview but the world.

# Creed for Atheists

Let us not speak of God
As if He were the nightmare of a naughty child,
Or a white lie for a widow,
Or a conscript's consolation on the battlefield.
Let us instead be awed
By the nothingness we've chosen not to be awed by,
The shade whose earthly shadow
We're standing in, the lie cast by a happy lie.
The face we turn away,
Let us turn it toward the others, let us find them out,
The ones who know the way
A sure thing looks when rounded with a little doubt,
The same ones every day
Who, kneeling all together in a common room,
Pray for their pets and pray
As well for us, their company in a common doom.
Let's take no satisfaction,
But concentrate on what we say when we say no:
That dead we are the same,
That time falls fast across the fading light like snow,
That man is an anxious motion
Of matter upon matter, liquor upon tongue,
The neurotransmitter's flame
Upon the dendrite's kindling — bright, and not for long.

# Poem Without Metaphors

Some days there are no other words for pain,
And for the worst, the literal is best:

The rain against the glass is only rain,
Your heart is just a muscle in your chest,

The book ends in a bookish sort of way,
The moonlight stands for nothing but the moon,

Your children carry half your DNA
And will inherit all your savings soon,

Somewhere a car is racing through the night
No faster than a swiftly moving car,

A brace of deer glance up at something bright —
Gone still, exactly like the deer they are.

And as for you, you could be anyone
Who's done, who's said, the things you've said and done.

# Drunk Lullaby

Quiet now, let's have a drink.
   Night withdraws beyond the door.
      No one needs another rhyme.
Cups and dishes brim the sink.
   Nothing matters anymore.

When the coin is cast again
   All the past will roll away,
      Humming on its reeded rim.
We will say of beauty then
   Everything there is to say.

Lift a parting glass and go
   Where good drinkers come to rest.
      Dream of whiskey, dream of rum.
We know all we need to know.
   Silence now is for the best.

# Last Call
# at the Conference Hotel

At two they were still married
To others asleep back home,
Talk having seldom varied
From her favorite epic poem.

They knew enough to keep shy
Of a nightcap in his suite,
Enough not to say goodbye
Or what year they might next meet.

She pulled away from his side
Just one of her sun-bright hairs
And laughed a last time, or tried,
And carried herself upstairs.

When she went, he turned to look
At his hands and raised no wave
And found the place in his book
He'd half-forgotten to save,

But a man roped to a mast,
By his oarsmen and his choice,
Aches to return when he's passed
The final, pitiless voice,

And sirens forget the sweet
Nothing as soon as it's sung,
And all one cannot repeat
Halters the heart with the tongue.

# Doubt

He's a god in my eyes,
Lesbia, the man you sit beside instead,
The one who rises when you rise,
Who shares a bed

With the same sweet, tipsy voice and laughter
That nightly consume
My senses and my sense, long after
You've left the room,

While my tongue lies flat in its cage
And my fingers fall slack
And the fire-bells in my skull rage
And both eyes go black.

Doubt, Catullus, ruins you,
The same doubt, at the same cost,
Kept by so many old kings, in lieu
Of the cities they lost.

# Lines on Evolutionary Psychology

How right it seems, just as it must have seemed
Right to relieve the feverish patient of
A quart of blood, back in the days men rhymed
  *Remove* with *Love*,

As right as drawing an answer from the guts
Some chicken gave up when the senate wanted
To worry out the most propitious dates
  For being haunted,

As right as charting, three degrees a night,
The rapturous, wrong orbits one beheld
When Earth was fixed in Man's and Heaven's sight
  And the center held,

As right back then as we today remain,
Constructing from some failure of the mind
The ancient threats our still-evolving brain
  Has left behind,

Since something almost human, far away
And unimaginably long ago,
Carried across the dangers of its day
  A pain we know.

# Trees at Night

They looked the same,
or nearly so, the trees,
ten million years ago,
in which our former
bodies stayed
thumb-footed, furred,
and unafraid, before
we ever fell awake
on mattress springs
no breeze could break
to watch the clock's
red numbers tame
a dark that hasn't
looked the same
since last we slept
in trees, above
that fall we're always
dreaming of.

# Ankou

Though nothing more than rumours now have touched
The little towns beyond the city walls,
And salted meats and vegetables yet hang
For sale in booths along the market street,
And still from every theatre ring out
The jeers and laughter of a lively pit,
And, just as ever, fools sic limping strays
Upon a bear chained, toothless, to a post,
And all the royals and all the nobles yet
Remain at court, untroubled by the crowds,
And nowhere have the roads begun to ooze
With naked almsmen heralding the End,
Still, every dawning day I search with dread
The loins and armpits of my little ones,
And every night before my second sleep
I look to all the windows of the house,
And hidden from the sleeping eye of Heaven
I gather bones and feathers in a bowl
And spare a drop of blood from my own palm
To purchase one more day of peace from Ankou.

This day some neighbor women came to call
And in my kitchen took their fill of ale,
And, mending in their laps, together drank
The blood-warm gossip of the wedding season,
The foreign gentles' sundry bad love-matches,
Some poor child's landed, liver-spotted groom,
The best and least of laces, flowers, and pies

Set forward by the families of those maids
Whose dowry chests and morning gifts were all
Our own not half a dozen years ago.
I smiled, no wiser than my witless friends.
But let one scratch her neck, or clear her throat,
My hand fled to my heart, and it was all
A Christian woman like myself could do
Not to take up a hot brand from the hearth
And screaming drive the lot into the street.

A Christian I am, never may you doubt.
I hearken to the priest, I say my prayers,
I school my little ones to trust the Lord,
I thank the Holy Mother for her Son
And ask her blessings on our lowly roof,
I show my back to Satan and his works,
And in sweet Christ I lodge my hope of Life.
But sweet Christ — Glory be to Him for ever —
Was born and slain a thousand leagues from here,
And in an alien desert He forgave
His killers in an alien desert tongue.
Christ lives, my only Saviour and my joy,
But far away in Heaven with his Saints,
While Ankou stalks the English countryside.

My mother's mother saw him as a girl.
One day in spring, when she was yet so young
Nobody feared that she should go astray,
She took herself alone into the woods,
And, toeing her way along a downed tree, faltered
And fell atop a body in a cart.
A beggar or a holy man, she thought,

And surely some days dead. But then he stirred.
His cowl, it slid a little from his face,
And well she marked the holes that were his eyes,
The lipless teeth that ranged his rotting smile,
The rising bony rustle of his laugh.
With not a word she hied herself back home.
A few days hence her kitchen cat fell sick.
Within a fortnight, half the town was dead.

I cannot say what frightens me the more,
That I devote my every second thought
To the propitiation of a Thing
Hateful to Christ and all of Christendom,
Or that I am the solitary soul
Who dreams all is not well. All is not well.
Beneath the shouts of vendors in the street,
He that hath ears may hear a different call,
A reedy tuneless keening on the wind,
That swells and fades and never disappears.
It is the call of Ankou's wooden cart,
The ancient axle stubborn with disuse,
The handles clacking at his skinless touch,
The wide bed which has always room for more.
Of late I hear it even in my sleep.
Empty for now, and nearer every day.

# The Dark Woods

They are still there, the dark woods from the dream,
While everything they symbolize is gone,
While the wireless speakers unwind their tidy theme
And the tiki torches stutter on the lawn,
While the dishwasher rattles the dishes in the sink
And the dog worries his tiny rubber man
And the blinking clocks aren't certain what to think
And the fruit fly circles back to where it began,
While the interest keeps the credit cards awake,
Collecting in a server states apart,
And the siren cries out for a stranger's sake
And the smartphone mutes its obsolescent heart,
While the box fan turns a bedroomful of breath
And the network brings the software up to date
And the skim milk dies a timely, painless death,
Still the woods, the woods you've dreamed about, they wait.

# An Organ
# of Extreme Perfection

We'll never know where every part is from,
Though it was from your mother's side you took
Your nose and second toe, and from mine come
Your cowlick and your constant worried look.

Most parts were passed down from some common place,
Mislaid by thirty-thousand years of snow,
Where a few last bear-skinned stragglers of the race
Fell quiet by the fire and turned to go.

Before that, other deaths shaped other parts:
Unlucky hunters spared you clumsy feet,
And a hundred billion slightly fainter hearts
Lost time against your own impatient beat.

But for now we lie and say all this was made
For you, as you seem dimly to believe,
While the days pass like a holiday parade
Of sights you'll learn to love, and then to leave.

The Author

Matthew Buckley Smith is the author of *Dirge for an Imaginary World* (Able Muse, 2012). His poems have been featured in *American Life in Poetry, Best American Poetry,* and *Poetry Daily.* He hosts the poetry podcast *SLEERICKETS* and lives in North Carolina with his wife and daughters.